IDEA

■ coaching pathway

Coaching the Person
(Instead of Just the Problem)

Terry B. Walling
Leader Breakthru

ENDORSEMENTS OF LEADER BREAKTHRU

"I was in the middle of a major role and organizational transition that I couldn't imagine navigating without the wise guidance of Leader Breakthru. Terry has brought clarity when the waters were murky and given me courage to stay the course when I was tempted to step back."

ROB YACKLEY, CREATOR OF THRESHOLDS

"The coaching and training from Leader Breakthru has transformed my approach to ministry. I would recommend to any person who is seeking clarity for their life to take advantage of the resources and the Spirit-led coaching approach that Leader Breakthru offers. I am deeply grateful for the coaching and leadership development in my own life and the lives of those in our church!"

ANDREW BURCHETT, LEAD PASTOR, NEIGHBORHOOD CHURCH OF CHICO

"The Leader Breakthru resources and coaching are fantastic. They are relevant for leaders at all levels who want to expand and deepen their Kingdom impact. Terry's facilitation and coaching skills are superb! His keen insights and inspiring passion provide the context and support to take one's leadership to the next level."

KIM ZOVAK, PCC COACH, TRAINER AND CONSULTANT

"Terry Walling's coaching and mentoring approach have been instrumental in my personal development and leadership. His work goes beyond technique and fads to get to the heart— what God is up to in a leader's life, shaping both doing and being for kingdom contribution."

DANIEL ALLEN, FOUNDER OF DANIEL ALLEN COACHING AND AUTHOR OF *SUMMONED*

"In the context of the coaching relationship, I have been empowered to discover with greater clarity my calling and contribution to advancing the Kingdom of God. Leader Breakthru's understanding of how God forms a leader has enabled me to partner with God in my own formation for the past 15 years."

ELAINE MAY, PASTOR OF MINISTRY LEADERSHIP, CHRISTIAN REFORMED CHURCH

"As a young leader, my life has been significantly impacted through the coaching and resources of Leader Breakthru. They coached me through a significant transition, and helped me better identify who I am as a leader. I am now taking these same Leader Breakthru tools to emerging leaders"

ZACK CURRY, JESUS CULTURE

"Leader Breakthru has helped resource hundreds of church, missional, and marketplace leaders all across Asia to gain clarity of their calling and contribution. The process is simple and amazingly powerful! A key resource for any leadership development pathway."

JOEL LAM, YOUTH WITH A MISSION, SINGAPORE

"Leader Breakthru's brand of coaching is becoming an invaluable resource for our churches as they make disciples. Focusing on the development of the leader, not just the skills of leadership—has had a tremendous impact on Mission Ohio."

STEVE HOPKINS, STATE CONVENTION OF BAPTISTS IN OHIO

"Leader Breakthru's coach training and leadership development will change the way you think and live out your calling as leaders. Leader Breakthru's training has given me a fresh perspective and transformed the way I develop leaders."

MARK MILLER, CHURCH PLANTER

"Leader Breakthru is a game-changer! The training and coaching were a life-changing experience that clarified my call, defined my role, and helped me identify my unique kingdom contribution."

DAVID MUNLEY, ASSISTANT PROFESSOR, NORTHPOINT BIBLE COLLEGE

"Leader Breakthru has significantly influenced my approach to assisting gifted leaders toward successful next steps as difference-makers. The coaching skills I have acquired have enabled me to facilitate leaders in discovering greater clarity for delivering a best contribution where they have influence."

ROBERT GRANT, COACH-SPEAKER, ANGLICAN MISSION

"Leader Breakthru has provided capable leadership, quality training, and excellent resources which has resulted in an effective coaching system for helping us develop the personal and professional lives of our leaders. We highly recommend them to you."

BRUCE PFADENHAUER, REGIONAL EXECUTIVE DIRECTOR, OPEN BIBLE CHURCHES

"After spending several years in personal transition, I became frustrated by my inability to clarify God's call. Leader Breakthru's coaching skills and training has provided me with the tools to discover God's direction in my life and lead others towards a similar awakening."

ALEX GILL, YOUTH MINISTER

"If you are looking for a holistic, God- honoring, development process, look no further than Leader Breakthru. What makes Leader Breakthru different? Terry and his team take seriously the fact that God has always been at work in your life and they leverage that in coaching.

JAMES WHATLEY, ASSOC. PASTOR, PEACE LUTHERAN

IDENTIFY

DISCOVER

EVALUATE

ACT

IDEA
■ coaching pathway

CONTENTS

Acknowledgements

Before Words by
Rob Yackley, Creator of Thresholds
Terry Walling, Founder of Leader Breakthru

ACKNOWLEDGMENTS

IDEA is the summation of thirty years of coaching and working alongside risk-taking, Kingdom leaders. Each coaching conversation has made a contribution to this new pathway. Special thanks goes to these friends.

Rob Yackley, for his ideation, word artistry, encouragement, and ministry partnership through the years. There is no greater friend, ministry warrior, and laughing partner than Rob. He lives the IDEA pathway as he coaches and leads *Thresholds* and leaders who are the architects of the new church.

Kyle Walling, who is more than just my son. He is my soul partner and one who is passionate to love God with his life. I am ridiculously proud of him. Kyle's heart for genuine faith, love for God, and his words of encouragement help birth my resources that serve leaders of all ages. Kyle is the graphic designer behind the IDEA model.

Christiana Rice, for her keen insights and editing additions to the manuscript. Christiana is one of today's best new leaders. Her counsel, coaching, and mentoring of leaders and their missional expressions is incredible. May her tribe increase.

Keith Webb, for all he has taught me and modeled in terms of coaching and giving more people access to coaching. The COACH model is an important inspiration behind the genesis of the IDEA pathway. Thanks Keith.

Steve Ogne, a brother we recently lost. Our loss is Christ's gain. Steve taught me early about coaching and partnering for Kingdom gain. Many of us owe our first days in coaching to Steve. When we all go home, the heroes will be different than here. Steve was a hero.

BEFORE WORDS

Rob Yackley, Creator of Thresholds
Co-Author, *Thin Places*

A few years ago I was staring straight into the face of one of the most significant vocational decisions I would ever make and there didn't seem to be a good way forward. If I stayed with the organization I had helped build and lead for almost 30 years, I would be choosing security and stability over passion and calling. If I left to begin something new, I would risk losing what we had created and possibly hurt a lot of people who I love deeply and had invested so much of my life into. Quite honestly, I was stuck.

In times of discernment, especially in times of decision-making that are particularly difficult, the Benedictines often ask 3 questions:

- Is it good for you?
- Is it good for us?
- Is it good for God's world?

I've always been pretty good at asking the second two Benedictine questions, but I don't often get around to asking the first one—at least not to myself. I regularly ask others what would be good for them, but it has always felt a bit selfish to ask myself what would be good for me. In the midst of this difficult vocational decision, I needed to ask myself that question and I needed to ask it in the presence of people who I trusted who had the spiritual sensitivity to affirm that it was okay—even necessary—to honestly listen to the longings of my heart. Terry was one of those trusted people I turned to.

Terry and I have been great friends, like-hearted dreamers, and ministry collaborators for almost 25 years, but in the midst of this grueling decision, I needed more than a friend—I needed a wise coach and Terry slid seamlessly into that role when I needed him the most.

The truth for many of us who lead is this: what is good for us personally—if we are tuned in to the Spirit of God—is usually good for those around us and ultimately good for the world. We don't always have to choose between what is good for us and what is good for the other. Terry helped me remember that and he helped me find the courage to lean into an unknown future that would give me life.

I share that story here because it highlights two pieces of the IDEA Coaching Pathway that I am particularly excited to see take a more prominent role in the coaching model. The first piece is the attentiveness to people and their personal development that is integrated into the IDEA model. Many coaching models are designed to help people get things done, (and that's certainly a good thing which the IDEA model delivers superbly!), but the development and the health of the person is primal in the IDEA model.

Secondly, I'm excited to see the IDEA model give coaches more freedom to offer wisdom and the gifts of their experience when they sense God prompting them to do so. The IDEA model still affirms conventional coaching wisdom, which holds that most answers are already in the coachee and it's the coach's job to pull them out. But the IDEA model creates space for coaches to sensitively share what they sense God doing and to offer what has been entrusted to them when the time is right.

Terry intuitively coaches with a compassionate emphasis on the person and a deep sensitivity to the nudging of the Spirit. Now he has a coaching model that will help the rest of us integrate those unique qualities with the best of conventional coaching wisdom and the world will be better for it!

Rob Yackley
2015

Rob Yackley is the co-author of *Thin Places: Six Postures for Creating and Practicing Missional Community* and is empowering missional community leaders throughout the country.

BEFORE WORDS

Terry Walling, Founder of Leader Breakthru
Author of *Stuck!* and *Awakening*

The competence of coaching is entering its
next chapter.

Coaching as a skill and profession has become
mainstream within both marketplace and ministry
vocations. It is a proven resource and skill impacting
those who seek solutions for their problems, insight for
their vocational questions and vision clarity for their
future. Coaching has demonstrated that the power of
listening and asking good questions has situation-
altering implications for leaders who proactively want to
implement change.

Yet the focus of coaching is shifting significantly.

Increasingly people are seeking out coaching for
reasons beyond problem-solving and vision crafting.
The coaching of tomorrow includes the development of
leadership character and personal growth. It moves
beyond career puzzles to the personal life and wellness
of the person for the sake of deep-rooted
transformation and authentic lives.

This adjustment to the focus of coaching precedes and
leads to lasting change in all sectors of society, no
matter one's vocation. The renewal of the person often
leads to new life and endeavors. This shift requires a
new set of questions and intentionality in the coaching.

When access to information, new ideas, and solutions
abound, what is needed now are innovative ways to
process what we know and translate its application not
only for the sake of the organization, but for the inner
life development of the person.

What you have in your hands is the result of over 30 years of integrating professional coaching and leadership development principles as an effective way of walking alongside Christ-centered leaders for the sake of their holistic development.

From leaders in local church expressions to new start-ups, to mission organizations or Christ followers who lead in marketplace settings, the IDEA coaching pathway is a proven model to generate significant impact. The IDEA pathway allows the coach not only to address the issues that people face on a day to day basis, but also to gain greater awareness of how these circumstances are shaping the inner life of the leader. Through this coaching process, leaders are awakened to God's on going formation in every aspect of their lives.

Breakthrough comes as we coach the person, not just the problem.

The IDEA coaching pathway is a series of intentional coaching steps, enhanced by a set of powerful questions that can help a coach to better listen and discern how the Spirit of God is at work, using each situation to shape the personal development of the person you coach.

God has created each individual with a unique purpose and calling, inviting us to align with God's plan for the world. The IDEA coaching pathway can help you and those you coach to better know and live out your ultimate contribution in the life God created us to live.

Terry Walling
2015

CHAPTER 1
THE IDEA COACHING PATHWAY

IDENTIFY
Identify with the person
Clarify the core desire

DISCOVER
Uncover the backstory
Surface the challenges

EVALUATE
Discern the Spirit's leading
Pinpoint the issue

ACT
Chart the next steps
Affirm the takeaways

After more than 20 years of coaching leaders, I thought it might be a good time to get some formal training on bettering my coaching skills. Yeah, I'm a quick study!

Up to this point, I was like most of us who are too busy doing the work of ministry to take time to develop ourselves. I learned ministry by doing ministry, picking up skills on the fly and reading the first 60 pages of too many books. I was the poster child for utilizing the famous "trial by fire" model in leadership development.

As I sat in a coach training event offered by Keith Webb and *Creative Results Management,* I realized that I was late to the game in terms of advancing my skills. I was deeply impacted by how God used the training to affirm my gifting, but also to take my coaching skills to a whole new level.

I had spent 14 years in pastoral ministry focused on solving problems…my own and others. People came to me for advice and answers, and it was my cultural duty to deliver. After those years, I spent the next 20 years resourcing pastors and church leaders in the area of leadership development. I felt especially called to those who were out on the edge, catalyzing change and renewal inside the existing church and outside traditional structures where fresh expressions were being pioneered.

I often felt the pressure of needing to have important responses and to deliver counsel that I thought others expected. I quickly discovered that one of the greatest gifts I could actually give leaders was a safe relational space to help them process the challenges they were confronting. I also began to discover that the posture of one who was one alongside, as co-learner, as opposed to one who took the posture of the consultant or expert, was more effective. Mine was a call to be like *Barnabas*, serving and coaching those I served, offering hope and encouragement that leaders rarely receive otherwise.

I was also learning that hope and new courage could emerge from the process of discovery. Giving the answers was about me. Framing the issues and facilitating discovery was about those I served. The result was often new and deeper knowledge and an increased passion for those leaders I coached.

These core lessons emerged for me:
• What a person or group discovers, they own.
• Whatever someone owns, they are more prone to implement.
• Whatever someone implements they will take responsibility for on a long-term basis.

The reverse of this is also seen:
• When someone is told the answer, ownership is often short-circuited causing them to not take responsibility for the implementation and the responsibility of change.
• If someone is mandated to implement another person's solutions, the results are also rarely good. They chafe under answers that are not their own, and typically do not pay the price required for implementation.

I became convinced that coaching and facilitating *discovery* is a core skill in helping catalyze change and foster the deep level of breakthrough that every leader needs. The more I experienced this first hand, the greater became my desire to learn more.

My early attempts at coaching felt rough and awkward. There were many moments when coaching looked more like "holy" manipulation than anything else. I would literally try to steer conversations toward *my* solutions for the problems I thought were most pressing. Trusting the person (or the Spirit in that person) to discover the answers on their own felt far too dangerous. Discovery meant that a loss of control for me, which is never a comfortable realization.

These early days brought me face to face with my propensity to over-talk and over-tell, robbing those I coached of the gift of listening and asking good questions Most whom I served were gracious and even allowed me to lead them down these near dead-end conversations. Yet the farther I went, the more I knew that the solutions were mine, and that there was very little ownership for real change. As the years progressed, I became convinced that there must be a better way.

Sitting in coach training with Keith Webb and *Creative Results Management,* I realized that I was limited in my skills as a coach. I had much to learn and I'm grateful for all the training I received that deeply enhanced my coaching skills and abilities.

Coaching has taught me that the power of discovery lies at the threshold of good, open, exploratory questions. The better the questions, the better the coaching and the greater the discovery.

I've learned that part of being a good coach or facilitator is letting go of control and trusting that the Spirit of God will guide the conversation into all truth.

I realized that my pattern in coaching was often to lead people down a haphazard way, or path toward what I thought was best for them. Many times, I would take those I coached on a "magical mystery tour" down a path that was clear to me, but unknown to them. Thanks to God's grace, we often got to good places in coaching but usually I had no idea how we actually got there.

As I was introduced to the idea of a "coaching path," I immediately saw my coaching again jump to a whole new realm of effectiveness. Embracing the idea of a coaching path, and adding structure to the coaching conversation, made my coaching much more productive. When the conversation took a detour, I was now able to get it back on course.

In my earlier yeas of coaching, the first coaching model/path I was exposed to was the **GROW** model, developed by Sir John Whitmore and documented in his book, *Coaching for Performance*. This book is a classic in the coaching world and is used to this day in business and sports coaching.

Whitmore's GROW model is a four-step coaching path involving four segments entitled: GOAL-REALITY-OPTIONS- WILL.

To me, the advantage of the GROW coaching path was that its acrostic framework is easy to remember, and the model acknowledges the need for a tangible goal as the end-result for each coaching conversation, before moving deeper into the coaching conversation.

The struggle with the GROW model was an understandable one. GROW places the emphasis on helping the person being coached to achieve whatever they desired. It was not a model focused around a person's spiritual life or ministry, so it was sometimes difficult to align the coaching with what God was doing in the inner life of the person. GROW was helpful, it is used by many Christian coaches, and it can work. But for our purposes,, it needed adaptation.

I was next introduced to the **COACH** model developed by Keith Webb at the training I mentioned earlier. Keith's book, *The COACH Model*, and his training, moved a step closer in terms of a coaching model for those in ministry. I like the COACH model and appreciate Keith's emphasis on coaching being a relational experience and his emphasizing on the Holy Spirit's role in the coaching.

COACH takes a person down a five-step path of CONNECT-OUTCOME-AWARENESS-COURSE-HIGHLIGHT.

My organization (Leader Breakthru) used the COACH model for several years. Keith works hard at making sure the model adapts to ministry leaders. We recommend Keith's book and insights on coaching as an important resource.

As we continued to coach and train ministry leaders, we began to recognize a significant, new trend. Our coaching conversations began to focus more and more on the individual's personal development and issues related to what holds a leader or individual back from living into their calling.

The desired goals/outcomes for the coaching conversations were shifting beyond questions of "how to deal with power brokers" or "how to cast vision" to deeper issues of character and defining moments in the shaping of the individual. The "presenting issue" often traces its way back down to the "real issue" related to what God is doing in the inner life.

Another observation in our use of COACH, and the coaching of those in ministry contexts were societal shifts and therefore shifts in church culture resulting in leaders experiencing major moments of personal transition. My book *Stuck!: Navigating Life and Leadership Transitions* was written to help those individuals (and their coaches) navigate these defining moments. The research of Dr. J. Robert Clinton in his book, *The Making of a Leader* reveals that transition periods are used by God to do some of His most important work in the development of leaders.

While the COACH model was helpful in these areas, there were times when we had to adapt the model to fit the developmental issues of the individual, and the coaching of ministry and mission leaders.

Our final discovery related to COACH further revealed that a possible change was needed as we realized that ministry leaders sometimes required a blend of coaching *and* mentoring. Often those we coached were in need of input from the coach. It became evident that the question was not whether input was needed, but when and how it occurred during the coaching.

In order to facilitate deeper breakthrough for those we coached, particularly helping coach ministry leaders and those they influenced, a modified coaching pathway was needed. We needed a more intentional path that could focus on the needs of the person—not just the problem--and where steps related to the discernment of God's shaping work, and input, were central.

The result was the birth of the **IDEA Coaching Pathway**. This intentional coaching path is designed to help coaches and those they coach to better address the issue at hand, but also to recognize, discern and align with God's deeper—and often greater—work.

Here are three reasons why the use of the **IDEA Coaching Pathway** might be of benefit for you and those you coach.

1. IDEA seeks to more intentionally focus on the person, not just the problems or issues they face.

IDEA begins with an identification with the person right from the start, and continues this emphasis throughout the coaching conversation. While IDEA can be used effectively in a non-ministry setting, the ministry sector benefits the most from the use of the IDEA Coaching Pathway. It is designed to integrate issues of personal development with coaching.

2. IDEA is easy to remember and use.

IDENTIFY *with the person and determine their core desire.*

Identify relates closely to the idea of coaching a real person and is linked closely to the *skill of listening.*

DISCOVER the backstory and surface the challenges.

Discover relates to the key focus of coaching—that is, personal discovery and ownership of the issue. This helps facilitate greater personal responsibility—and it is linked closely to the *skill of expanding.*

EVALUATE what the Spirit is at work doing and pinpoint the issue.
Evaluate helps correspond to the issue of pinpointing the option that most addresses the "real" issue that the Spirit has started to reveal, and it better relates closely to the *skill of focusing.*

ACT to address the issue and summarize the takeaways.

Act emphasizes the need for obedience and behavior, demonstrating the importance of putting faith into action. It relates closely to the *skill of empowering.*

- Four steps are easier than five or six
- The four words of IDEA clearly describe the function of each of the four steps of the path

- Each step of the IDEA path is tied to one of the core coaching skills (listening, expanding, focusing, and empowering), allowing for greater clarity in the function required to achieve that step

3. The IDEA coaching pathway brings discernment to the forefront of the conversation and helps to pinpointing the critical issue.

Like Jethro's defining moment with Moses in Exodus 18:1-18, the "actual" reason for the coaching conversation may shift from the need for a new management style to the leader going to a new place with God and in his or her leadership.

The EVALUATION step in the IDEA pathway provides an intentional moment to focus on discerning the one issue (the "jugular") that could lead to breakthrough. The pinpointing of this issue involves the discernment of how the Spirit is at work, (John 16:13), along with issues related to how God shapes his people (leadership development).

It's important to note that the intent of the IDEA Coaching Pathway is not to turn every coaching conversation into a conversion moment.

Not every coaching conversation requires deep spiritual processing, or going after issues of personal development. Nor does IDEA seek to focus only on spiritual formation. The growth of spiritual direction in the West has risen up to serve that need. But, by setting up a path to include the potential of addressing these issues, IDEA does allows for a coaching conversation that often is better able to get to the real struggles. If issues of personal development now need to surface, they have a path to facilitate those interactions.

Closing Thoughts

- All models focus on essential things
- Each model offers unique advantages
- No one model is inherently better than another

> **The critical question is...**
> **what's the goal of the coaching?**

If the goal of your coaching is to empower spiritual leaders to better live into God's purposes and plans for their lives, then IDEA offers a significant advantage.

The next chapter introduces four key postures that foster greater effectiveness when using IDEA.

CHAPTER 2
FOUR POSTURES

At Leader Breakthru, we train coaches to coach and to integrate leadership development into their coaching.

Every time we're introducing coaching to ministry leaders, we hear a collective sigh of relief from those attending.

The sighs occur when we first share that our assumption for those attending the training is that they are already coaching. When anyone comes alongside another person and helps serve their needs and bring clarity to their walks with Christ, coaching is inevitable. The IDEA training seeks to help them better understand coaching and enhance their coaching skills.

Secondly, those at our training further relax when we affirm that coaching *is* ministry. Coaching in the ministry context is really about "voice recognition." It's helping those you coach better recognize the voice of the Spirit.

There are so many voices competing for the attention of each of us. The ministry of coaching is about helping those we lead and serve to align their lives better with the God of love. Coaching is about hearing Christ's voice and following.

> *"But they never will follow a stranger; in fact, they will run away from him because his sheep follow him because they know his voice."*
> *—John 10:5 (NIV)*

BENEFITTING FROM THE IDEA COACHING PATHWAY

The IDEA Coaching Pathway seeks to position the conversation between the coach and coachee to address the presenting, or known issue, but also to better discern God's leading and potentially the deeper issue that is surfacing in and through the situation.

• IDEA is fueled by four postures
• A posture refers to an attitude or approach that helps produce a desired end result

IDEA makes its greatest contribution to the coaching conversation as the coach:

• holds a sovereign mindset
• believes in the potential of breakthrough
• recognizes the power of aligning to Christ
• and believes that coaching is ministry

One of the distinguishing features of coaching is that the one being coached is the one who sets the agenda for the coaching conversation. The truth is, though, that for those who follow Christ, there is often another agenda. The felt need and desired outcome of the coaching conversation takes a back seat to the real issue that God is seeking to address.

> *We coach the person and work the problem.*
> *We don't coach the problem and work the person.*

Good coaches care for the deeper needs of the person as they seek to address the agenda of the one they coach. Most coaches would agree and they seek to include the needs of the person in their coaching. But If the evaluation of an effective session comes from problem-solving alone, it is possible to miss a significant opportunity to cultivate a person's spiritual formation. God may have brought that person to you, as a coach, for something more than solving a problem.

> *Jim and I were deep into our coaching conversation before we realized that God was using this coaching conversation to challenge his trust and confidence in God's call on his life. We had come to talk about how to determine on where he would go next, and his personal vision, and we ended up focusing on Jim's struggle to go to a deeper level of trust in God's right to have control of his life. At the end of the conversation we were both astounded at how the coaching went a completely different direction than we both thought it would go. Jim was very thankful that it did.*

Each of the four postures below help to build resolve in the coach and set the stage in the coaching environment to see God able to use the coaching to minister to the person more than addressing the problem.

POSTURE #1: SOVEREIGN MINDSET
GOD OFTEN USES THE PRESENTING ISSUE TO SURFACE THE REAL ISSUE

We typically live situationally, yet God calls each of us to live sovereignly.

There has never been a time when God hasn't been at work. The question isn't whether God is at work; the question is: what is God at work doing? And the even greater question is: do we, God's people, have the courage to join God's work? (Romans 8:32 (NIV), 2 Peter 1:4 (NIV), Ephesians 2:8-10 (NIV).

God uses people, events, and circumstances to shape our lives. Entering the coaching conversation with the awareness of God's sovereign, shaping work opens the coach up to see the potential of God's greater work as revealed by the Holy Spirit, who leads and guides both coach and coachee to all truth (John 16:13, NIV). The IDEA Coaching Pathway creates moments in the conversation for God's intentional shaping work to surface.

IDEA is designed to help you stay alert to God's sovereign purposes. The pathway grants you the freedom to follow the deeper work God could be doing.

POSTURE #2: COACHING + MENTORING
BREAKTHROUGH COMES THROUGH COACHING WITH PERIODIC MENTORING

Most who refer to coaching actually mean mentoring.

Mentoring has to do with depositing something in the person you seek to help. Coaching stands alongside and draws insights out through personal discovery.

> **Coaching pulls things out.**
> **Mentoring puts things in.**

Over the years, I've listened to the concerns within the coaching ranks to not biasing the coaching conversation with input or the views of the coach. While I subscribe to the coachee setting the agenda and the overall coaching posture, there does come a time when the coach needs to deposit new information that is not attainable in any other way except from the coach.

Concise input brought into the conversation at a strategic moment allows the coaching and the person being coached to not plateau or remain stuck in their current paradigms. I find this particularly true when it comes to ministry coaching. Many of those who approach a coach are wanting the input of the coach (i.e., they want mentoring).

It's helpful not to jump automatically to mentoring and the "telling" mode, but instead to offer input while maintaining a coaching posture. At strategic moments in the conversation, coaches can switch "hats" to that of a mentor, advisor, or spiritual guide, and then return to a coaching posture. This moving in and out of the coaching posture is an art, not a science, and is learned over time with practice.

If advice, counsel, and/or new information are offered too soon in the conversation, those being coached are robbed of the power of discovery and ownership of the issue. However, if the mentoring is offered at the right time, it's possible to see the conversation move forward with the coachee still setting the agenda and taking responsibility for the issue.

The IDEA coaching pathway helps coaches find the right time for feedback in the coaching conversation as well as learn how feedback can help determine the options for the next steps forward.

POSTURE #3: THE POWER OF ALIGNMENT
GOD IS ALREADY AT WORK, SO COACHING IS ABOUT ALIGNING WITH GOD'S WORK

In John 5:19-23 (NIV), we find Jesus surrendering to the will of the Father and the Father revealing to the Son what He is at working doing (v. 20). In his humanity, Jesus models the act of surrender and aligning himself with God to discover God's plans and purposes.

As coach and coachee make the choice to align with God's work, they are positioned in greater ways to see God's work. The Father does the same work today revealing through the ministry of the Holy Spirit the plans and will of the Son and the purposes and plans already at work.

The prize of surrender is revelation.

Ephesians 2:10 tells us the Father, Son, and Spirit ordained good works for each of us to do before time began. It's not a question of God working through the circumstances, events, and people we confront each day; instead, it's more about how bad do each of us want to see and know God's work. Like the Son, are we willing to lay down our agendas in order to see what is on God's heart?

It almost goes without saying, but this isn't a formula or way for the coach to move to the telling mode. Instead, when coaches and coachees choose to surrender their own agendas something more can happen in the coaching conversation beyond just solving a problem.

POSTURE #4: THE IMPACT OF DISCOVERY
GOD USES THE COACHING RELATIONSHIP TO DEEPEN OWNERSHIP OF HIS WORK

The fourth posture that foster increased impact from use of the IDEA Coaching Pathway is a high commitment to the need for discovery.

Coaches ask questions to draw out assumptions, identify motivations, surface paradigms, and reveal self-limiting beliefs. Coaching is done with a bias and assumption that most answers are within the person being coached. The role of the coach is to draw them out. The greater the articulation by the coachee of the issue, the greater the potential for discovery.

The IDEA Coaching Pathway intentionally focuses the early efforts of the coaching conversation on the importance of discovery. More than just gaining an awareness of the issues, the early questions and looking at the topic from a diversity of angles promotes discovery and future ownership of the change that will be needed.

Focus and ownership are tied to articulation.

The answers one seeks are often within. Solutions are realized in the midst of discovery. IDEA helps promote discovery and increases the ability of those being coached to take responsibility for their behavior and formation.

- In chapters 3-6, each step of IDEA is described and example questions are given
- In chapter 7, the link between coaching and leadership development is explained
- In chapter 8, you'll find ways to utilize IDEA as you coach and to use IDEA to build a coaching culture

CHAPTER 3
STEPPING STONE ONE
IDENTIFY

*"Do not merely look out for your own personal interests,
but also for the interests of others."*
—Philippians 2:4

The first stepping stone of the IDEA Coaching Pathway is to IDENTIFY with the person and help determine the core desire and end-result of the coaching session.

> ***Identify* with the person**
> ***Clarify* the core desire**

The two segments of **IDENTIFY** are interrelated. By identifying first with the person, the coach gains invaluable insights which help clarify the core desire for the coaching conversation.

IDENTIFY WITH THE PERSON

Coaching is relational. It's the connection between the coach and the person being coached that builds a bridge to something more.

IDEA coaching begins by investing time to identify with the person being coached, learning their current situation, and building an intentional connection with them first as a person. It's an authentic hearing of real life—the challenges, ups and downs, and getting a current read on life and its demands. It's about building rapport and trust. This step isn't a means to an end, but rather a genuine expression of interest on behalf of the coach to enter the world and establish a genuine relational connection.

Entering into the world of the coachee can often be blocked by the noise in the coach's life. Identifying with the person is a discipline of valuing a person enough to see the world from his or her perspective.

In their book, *Co-Active Coaching*, Henry KImsey-

House, Phil Sandahl, and Laura Whitworth express this identification as Level Three coaching. Level One is seeing the coachee's world through your perspective. Level Two is about the coach asking questions about the coachee's world in order to better understand it. Level Three is about the coach sitting alongside the individual and examining the world and the issues with the coachee, viewing it from their perspective and seeking to understand even what isn't being said. That takes discipline.

> *Zack is a fast-paced, high-achieving young leader. Our coaching appointments are important to him to be able to have a time and a for personal focus. Our IDENTIFY time is vital, and often lengthy, as he unpacks all that has occurred since our last coaching appointment. I often ask him how he's doing, and he is off to the races, putting all the challenges, questions, desires, and frustrations out on the table.*
>
> *At some point, Zack will stop, catch his breath, and smile. Then ask me, "So what do you think?" I love looking at him and asking, "What do you think?" The coaching has already begun.*

In my early days of coaching, I often jumped in and picked an early issue that I felt was important to a leader, or picking something I felt comfortable to help with, launching the discovery process far too early. We would often have to backtrack to get to the real issue. Now that I'm more comfortable with the coaching process and do not feel the need to fix people and their problems. I see the value in listening and using these early moments to place myself into a leader's world.

In this beginning segment, coachees will surface a variety of things related to lives and their current circumstances. These life situations may not be, in the end, the topic of the coaching conversation, but they're invaluable for the coach to know as background for the issues that will be discussed. Though this first segment seems to be a natural segue into coaching, effective coaching has actually already started when we identify with the person.

This first segment also signals the launch of the spiritual connections that occur between the Holy Spirit, the coach, and the person being coached. There are three different kinds of conversations occurring in the coaching relationship when God is involved:

- The conversation between the coach and coachee is a *dialogue* related to known issues and current perceptions.

- The conversation between the coach and the Spirit is one of *discernment* and seeks to attune the coach to the work of God.

- The conversation between the coachee and the Spirit of God is one of *direction,* where the Spirit begins the process of both revealing and guiding the process of discovery,

Here are some examples of IDENTIFY questions that help to identify with the person:

- How have you been?
- How are things?
- How does life feel right now?
- How's work? Home? Kids? Church? Ministry?
- What are some challenges right now?
- How's your schedule looking right now?

CLARIFY THE CORE DESIRE

At some point, the conversation begins to shift into the second segment of the IDENTIFY stepping stone as the coach begins asking questions that seek to identify the individual's core desire for the coaching conversation.

One of the keys for the IDEA Coaching Pathway is time invested in identifying the coachee's core desired outcome for the coaching conversation. What distinguishes a helpful time of dialogue and an effective coaching conversation is gaining clarity on the outcome for that conversation early on. Getting the core desire clear and upfront helps make the coaching impactful and provides a guide for the coach as he or she manages the coaching conversation. Surfacing the core desire often begins as the coach asks the simple question:

"What would be most helpful to talk about in our time together today?"

> *Bryan always comes ready. He knows I'll ask him the question related to his desire and goal for our coaching time, so he typically takes his first shot at a desired outcome.*
>
> *The core desire in my coaching with Bryan rarely ends up to be the topic we focus on. Not because Bryan is wrong, or because I set the agenda for the coaching, but because Bryan is like most people who come to coaching knowing they need a coaching conversation, but not all that clear on what their core desire is for the coaching. Investing time is clarifying the core desire is essential.*

Only after the coach and coachee explore potential topics does the most pressing core desire surface. The agreed-upon end-result for the coaching conversation should exhibit three characteristics:

- It needs to be *specific* so that both coach and coachee are clear and know what they are going after
- It needs to be *intelligible* in that it is understandable to both coach and the coachee so they know when the goal has been accomplished
- It must be *time-sensitive,* attainable to be achieved in the time the coachee and coach have allotted for the coaching conversation

Specific • Intelligible • Time-sensitive (SIT). I tell myself that it's better to **SIT**, linger, and even wait until the core-desire is clarified before proceeding. The better both understand the real, core desire, the more real and effective the coaching conversation.

> *The person being coached sets the agenda for the coaching conversation. The agenda or desired outcome is called the "core desire."*

One of the first advantages of the IDEA Coaching Pathway is bringing legitimacy to the investment into the person and the relationship. Helping the individual sort out and sort through what would be most helpful to talk about is linked to Level Three listening and identifying with the person

Example of IDENTIFY questions that help to surface core desire could include:

- What would be most helpful to talk about in our time together?
- What's a core issue that you would like to go after in our time?

- What would be most helpful for us to address?
- What could we talk about today that would make the most difference in your journey or situation right now?

The first stepping stone of IDEA begins the process of building relational trust between the coach and the person being coached. Coaching often sinks or swims based upon the level of trust in the coaching relationship. The coachee needs to feel that their coach is able to identify with them as a person and has their best interest at heart.

A Note: Supervisors can be coaches, but it's important that the individual being coached is assured that the organization and its needs, or the coach's desires for the person, take second chair. One way to distinguish that is through clarifying which "hat" the coach is wearing. More on this later.

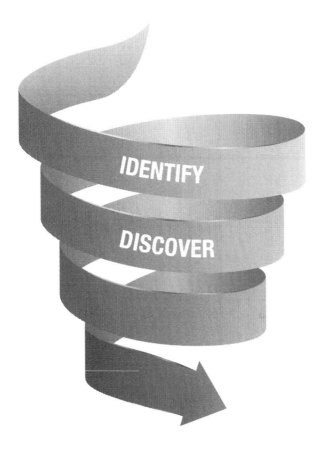

*"The purposes of a person's heart are deep waters,
but one who has insight draws them out."*
—**Proverbs 20:5 (NIV)**

The second stepping stone in the IDEA Coaching Pathway involves the use of pure, open questions and active listening to DISCOVER the essential story behind and around the issue being explored.

> ***Uncover* the backstory**
> ***Surface* the challenges**

As background information about an issue is shared and the circumstances are unpacked, the coachee becomes aware of the challenges they face and their own ability to address them.

There are two segments to the DISCOVER step in the IDEA pathway, and these steps tend to be sequential. As the coach better understands the situation and additional information reveals the backstory related to the topic, the coach and coachee can better identify what the coachee is up against.

UNCOVER THE BACKSTORY

To uncover the story behind the story, expanding questions that are open, pure, empathetic, and probing in nature are required. Coaches often need a diversity of questions in order to take a multi-angle approach to discovery. Don't rush towards solutions too soon. Maintaining a discovery posture as long as possible helps provide more information and build greater ownership for future decision-making and change.

> *Change happens as soon as the*
> *first question is asked.*

Sonja often comes to the coaching very prepared. She knows what she wants to go after, and typically has her questions or thoughts about a topic ready to share. What she really needs from me as a coach is letting her be free to share and explore her thinking. She needs a safe-place and a coach secure enough to let her share her thinking.

What often occurs is that as she hears herself begin to unpack the issues, her discovery of the obstacles or challenges surface. As she tests her thinking, she herself begins to hear the weak spots and loopholes in her logic. If I can remain asking questions, she often arrives at the answers on her own.

The temptation is to jump too quickly into identifying the obstacles or problems the coachee is facing without giving them the freedom to explore. Early questions often need to focus on helping the coachee look at the issue from multiple angles. Like examining a rare stone or gem, the coach needs to help the coachee examine the topic from a series of coaching angles through good questions.

The coach's focus is to expand the awareness of the issue during this first part of discovery.

Example of DISCOVER questions that help to provide key information and uncover the story could include:

- Where would you like to start?
- What issues do you feel would be most helpful to talk about as we begin to explore this issue?
- Talk about what you see as the keys related to this core issue we are trying to address.
- What are the circumstances that are contributing to this?

- What do you see to be some of the other factors that are driving this?
- What are the factors you have bumped into in the past as this has surfaced?

SURFACE THE CHALLENGES

Good coaching challenges assumptions and often helps reveal self-limiting beliefs.

As discovery continues, I will often send out what I call "coaching probes." I do this by using statement questions to see how the coachee responds, and if what they are saying is true to actual reality. Probes often sound like this:

- "Really?"
- "Do you buy what you are saying?"
- "I think you already know the answers to this!"
- "Is that what your spouse or closest friends would say?"
- "Are you sure you really believe that?"

The backstory often uncovers issues that aren't being talked about. As the coach leans in, issues of self-limiting beliefs and past struggles begin to emerge. As the coachee responds, they and the coach begin to see potential obstacles and challenges to forward progress.

> *Jeff had hit a crossroads moment in his life direction and needed to make an important shift in focus and jobs. His current ministry was effective, but limiting in terms of future options. As we worked through the DISCOVER process, it was obvious to me that Jeff knew what he needed to do, but he kept deferring to me for advice.*

"I think you already know what you are suppose to do Jeff," I stated. "You are just are afraid to admit it to yourself?" I continued.

"You really think so?" was Jeff's response.

"What do you think is really occurring here?" I asked. Out came Jeff's desire and his fear of stepping into the unknown.

One of the core gifts that the coach brings to the conversation is helping the coachee synthesize their insights into points of challenges or obstacles. This is often done by paraphrasing and even laser phrasing the responses. This helps to crystallize roadblocks and stimulates deeper questioning. Ten minutes of interaction can be boiled down to a one-sentence summation—for example, "Our challenge is not what to do, but the fear to step out and do it," as was the case with Jeff.

In the DISCOVER step, the coach isn't looking to address the answer to the problem, but to identify the obstacles or challenges the coachee is facing.

The outside perspective of the coach, and the questions he or she asks, often surface blind spots to the coachee. A blind spot is a significant truth that can be seen by others, but remains unknown to the person being coached. As the questions continue to unfold, the coachee begins to not only discover the issues, but recognize the need for change.

DISCOVER is also the place where the coach begins to surface questions related to how God might be at work in this current situation. Reviewing past experiences where God has used similar situations to shape issues of character and obedience becomes appropriate and helpful. How God is at work may be a blind spot to the coachee.

Example of DISCOVER questions that help to surface the challenges the coachee is facing, and the work of God could include:

- When you've gotten here before, what have been some of your responses?
- As you listen to yourself, what are you hearing to be your significant challenges?
- What do you see to be the key obstacles that are holding you back?
- What could move you and this situation forward?
- What haven't we talked about that's important?
- What have others said to you in terms of being key to this issue?

CHAPTER 5
EVALUATE

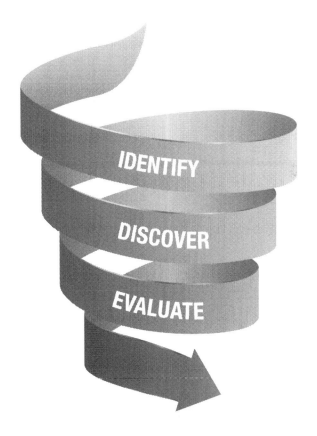

*"Trust in the L*ORD *with all your heart and lean not on your own understanding; in all your ways submit to him, and he will make your paths straight."*

—**Proverbs 3:5-6 (NIV)**

The IDEA Coaching Pathway now moves to the final stepping stone of the coaching conversation and into a time of pinpointing the actual issue that the coachee discovers that they need to address.

EVALUATE is more than just weighing out the options. It's a discerning process when coach and coachee seek to identify the "jugular" issue that, if addressed, will bring potential breakthrough to the situation and release new hope and momentum.

Discern the Spirit's leading
Pinpoint the issue

The two segments of the EVALUATE stepping stone in the IDEA Coaching Pathway work in tandem, offering checks and balances for each other.

The coach continues to use questions to identify the core issue that needs to be addressed and clarity is cultivated as coach and coachee seek to discern the Spirit's work. Feedback from the coach is often a key element in the conversation.

The third stepping stone down the IDEA pathway is more than just a review of the potential issues that need to be addressed. Instead, it's when the individual needs to be challenged to own the issue and take responsibility to focus and respond. If the results of EVALUATE are achieved, it sets up the final step in the IDEA journey.

DISCERNING THE SPIRIT'S LEADING

God uses a variety of people, events, and circumstances to shape people's character and their influence. What appears on the surface to be a simple problem or concern may be a time when God is actually at work forming the inner life. This time of discernment in the coaching conversation offers a unique contribution in the IDEA Coaching Pathway.

Processing moments that often occur in a Christ-followers life include:

- Integrity Checks
- Obedience Checks
- Faith Challenges
- Isolation Processing
- Negative Preparation
- Leadership Backlash

The question isn't whether God is at work; the question is what is God at work doing and do we have the courage to join God?

Kyle was struggling to really know why he felt that he needed to make an important shift in his ministry. Intuitively he knew what he needed to do, but not clear on what was driving the decision. As we walked through the issue, God was using this decision to help crystallize his values. In fact this decision was really an integrity check.

My coaching questions focused on helping him see deeper into his circumstance.

What do you think is driving your thinking?

> *What do you feel God is seeking to clarify through this decision?*
> *What values does this issue surface?*

What appeared to be an issue or need for a new skill or an answer on how to handle an important issue can often—but not always—reveal itself to be more. As coach and coachee continue to dialogue, they may begin to see God's deeper and greater work.

For coaches, it's critical to maintain a listening posture to what the Spirit may be saying and doing. But what the *coachee* senses God is doing is most important. If feedback by the coach is needed, it's important that the coach "go slow" with the sharing. Spiritual feedback should be done succinctly, in humility, and offered as a "potential way" God may be at work.

Knowing and discerning the actual issue is a result of both coach and coachee sensing what the issue might be, and how God is at work.

Examples of EVALUATE questions that help to discern how the Spirit could be at work could include:

- How do you see God at work in all of this?
- What are you hearing in terms of God's desires for you in all of this?
- What issue of character might this be touching?
- How does all of this fit with what you see God doing shaping you? Your leadership?
- Talk about how God might be using this to clarify your influence as a leader.
- What areas might this be touching in regards to struggles or wounding?

(Note: For more helps, see Chapter 7, *Coaching and Leadership Development*)

PINPOINTING THE ISSUE

Surfacing and sifting through a variety of issues and challenges help identify the central issue and challenge the coachee is facing. It's critical that good questions still be used to pinpoint the essential area to focus attention. The micro-skill of pinpointing what that issue might be needs to be the focus of this portion of the IDEA pathway.

The coach and coachee are looking to identify the jugular issues. The jugular is the place of attack, where if a strike can be made, the whole of the issue can be impacted.

> **The "Jethro Moment" is when the jugular issue emerges in the conversation revealing what needs to be addressed.**

The coach continues in a listening posture, but as he or she listens, it might become apparent that feedback is needed.

Self-evaluation is always the best form of feedback. Allowing the coachee to have "first crack" at what needs to be addressed, and giving themselves their own input, is by far the most beneficial way for feedback to occur.

John Whitmore, author of the book *Coaching for Performance*, offers these important insights:

> "Generating high quality, relevant feedback, as far as possible, from within rather than from the experts is essential for continuous improvement at

work, in sport, and in all aspects of life" (p. 33).

"If I give you my advice and it fails, you blame me. I have traded my advice for your responsibility, and that is seldom a good deal" (p. 37).

The goal of feedback by the coach is to provide the coachee with helpful, needed, and strategic information in the conversation. Many things could warrant feedback, but what's the most important thing? Feedback often provides new insights to existing thinking, and can help to shift the paradigms in order to generate new answers to old problems.

> *Typically I ask a permission question before I launch in to giving feedback: "Are you ready for a comment?" or "Are you up for some feedback?"*

> *Rick was ready. I sought to be both concrete and as specific as I could be.*

> *"I think this is not an issue of vision. I think it is more of an issue of you believing you can take the church to a new place, as opposed to the wording of the vision. Once you go there, I think the way to communicate the vision will follow."*

Premature feedback can risk robbing the individual of ownership of the issue. Rightly timed feedback can lead to the desired breakthrough.

One way that the coach can make the transition from listening and asking to the role of offering feedback and giving input is through the mental picture of "changing hats." The coach first gains permission to provide feedback. They take off the coach hat and put on the mentor/advisor hat. In giving feedback, three keys should be kept in mind:

- Be specific
- Use concrete examples to help illustrate
- Never try to convince, but rather offer information for consideration

The most important moment in the giving of feedback comes in making sure the coach returns to the coaching posture—putting the coaching hat back on signals the need to process the information shared, and helps the individual being coached to have the freedom to process the relevance of the feedback.

Example of EVALUATE questions that help to pinpoint the issue and the way forward could include:

- What are you hearing in all of this?
- If you were to sum up our discussion, what would you say is the issue that you need to address?
- How would you evaluate what you need to do?
- If you were to pinpoint the problem or issue, what do you think it is?
- Of all that you could address, what do you think is the most important for you to go after?
- If you were me, what would you be telling the person you were coaching?

CHAPTER 6
STEPPING STONE FOUR
ACT

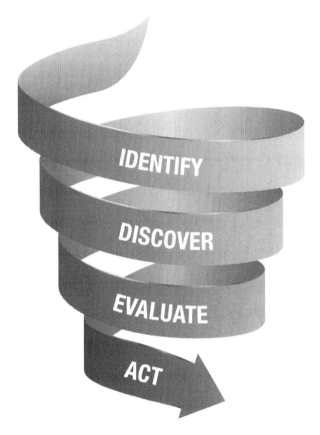

"You did not choose me, but I chose you and appointed you so that you might go and bear fruit— fruit that will last—and so that whatever you ask in my name the Father will give you."
—John 15:16 (NIV)

The final stepping stone in the IDEA Coaching Pathway is ACT. Its focus is on determining the steps of action that will put new behavior to the insights gained, as well as help coach and coachee affirm the gains and insights from the coaching conversation.

> **Chart the next steps**
> **Affirm the takeaways**

The two parts to the ACT portion of the IDEA pathway help bring closure to the discussion by moving beyond talk to action by charting the next steps forward and bringing closure to the conversation by affirming the key takeaway.

> *Coaching is about action, not just reflection.*

CHART THE NEXT STEPS

The IDEA Coaching Pathway moves into action by helping the coachee develop one to two strategic action steps to address the jugular issue that resulted from the evaluation step. Charting the next steps is about identifying the few, important steps that can catalyze change now, as well as new behavior over a longer period of time.

The next days are important days as the coachee leaves the coaching conversation. What they choose to do next will give great insight to the impact of the coaching. The first 100 days of any desired change are crucial. If something tangible can occur within the first 100 days following a major breakthrough, there is a greater potential for new behavior.

SMART action steps are often the first baby-steps to long-term change. The establishing of Strategic • Measurable • Achievable • Relevant • Time-framed goals or actions steps can provide short-term wins and ignite new momentum.

> *Allen knew what he needed to do. But taking the step to do it meant stepping over the line and putting feet to his decision.*
>
> *"What do you think you need to do to put this into action?" I asked.*
>
> *"This is where it get's hard," Allen responded. "I don't know how everyone will respond," Allen continued.*
>
> *"How about we just step this out with some action steps you can measure, and then see how it goes?" I asked.*
>
> *"Often times we get too far down the track, figuring out all the variables, that we don't act at all. I continued. Give me one, strategic next step, that is aligned with what you know God wants, and one that we can both measurable and fits within our time frame?"*

SMART action steps are:

- *Strategic*: It's a behavior goal that addresses the jugular issue

- *Measurable*: It's a tangible behavior goal that when it is achieved in can be recognized

- *Achievable*: It has the potential of being accomplished in a reasonable period of time

- *Relevant*: It's a behavior goal that directly relates to the issue that needs to be addressed

- *Time-framed*: It has a deadline and offers accountability in terms of completion

When charting action steps, the coach now begins to use questions to help the individual arrive at action steps that are SMART. It's crucial that the action steps come from the coachee. Authorship of action is tied to ownership of action.
Example of ACT questions that help to ensure SMART action steps could include:

- What actions do you feel you need to take to move this issue forward?
- Which one of two steps do you feel would be most strategic in addressing the issue?
- Are these goals achievable given your current situation and time availability?
- In what way are these goals tied to helping us address what we need to go after?
- How will you know when you are working against this step?

AFFIRM THE TAKEAWAYS

The IDEA Coaching Pathway reaches its completion with the ensuring of accountability and the summation of takeaways from the coaching conversation.

The final challenge from the coach is to help the individual establish self-initiated accountability for the action steps that have been created. If the coaching includes multiple conversations, the coach is sometimes the one holding the coachee accountable for their action, by setting up accountability question that will be asked at the next coaching session.

If the coaching session is a one-time event, the coach helps the coachee set up an accountability structure that the coachee will actually utilize.

Coaching builds increased self-awareness.

Asking the coachee for his or her takeaway from the session helps both the individual and coach summarize what insights were gained. Genuine affirmation by the coach should follow summation of the takeaway(s) with the coach offering encouragement to the coachee for efforts made, and the willingness to be vulnerable and grow as a Christ-follower and leader.

The value of naming the takeaway also helps the coach and coachee be able to recognize the growing self-awareness occurring within the individual—another residual of IDEA and the result of coaching the person, not just the problem.

> *As I sought to bring our coaching to a close, Alex responded to my question related to what was most helpful from our coaching conversation:*
>
> *"Without a doubt it was helping me come to the point of seeing what I needed to do. I now know why God wants me to stay put, and how all these things I have been feeling point to me not heading home, but heading off to school. Thanks for the help."*
>
> *"I am really proud of you and the way you worked through all this. It would have been pretty tempting to go back to where all your support base is, as opposed to follow God in all of this! Way to go!"*

Example of ACT questions that help to affirm the takeaway could include:

- What is one question that someone can ask you to help you stay on track?
- How can I (or others) best help you stay accountable for your action steps?
- What's one takeaway from our time together today?
- What was your highlight from our time together?
- What part of our coaching conversation was most important to you and for you today

CHAPTER 7
COACHING AND LEADERSHIP DEVELOPMENT

You don't get to clarity alone.

Coaching is a relational experience in which one person facilitates an individual or group to discover their God-given potential, so that they may grow personally in the intimacy with Christ and make their unique Kingdom contribution for Christ.

Coaching is about facilitating discovery rather than delivering content. The coachee is the expert on their own life. Coaching is about the individual and leader as a person—not just about adding new skills or knowledge that provide the potential of being successful.

Coaching is about change and confronting limitations, habits, thought patterns, and blind spots often deeply embedded over the years. Coaching provides the greater potential over time.

You learn to coach by (1) being coached, and (2) by coaching others.

Leadership development is the study of influence over a lifetime. At its core, leadership is about influence, not title or position or salary. Christ-centered leadership development is the study of how God shapes the influence of a leader over a lifetime.

Dr. J. Robert Clinton, author of *The Making of a Leader*, defines a Christian leader as one who has been entrusted with God-given capacities and God-given responsibilities to *influence* people to fulfill God's purposes. God shapes a Christ-follower and their influence by using people, events, and circumstances to develop character and skills (Psalm 78:72; Mark 3:13-15). Every believer will go through a series of phases in their development with key transitions along the way that keep an individual moving forward.

When coaching meets leadership development, something unique occurs: insight meets processing, information meets transformation, and a Christ-follower becomes a leader as they discover God's sovereign, shaping work.

Coaching + Leadership Development = Breakthrough

Breakthrough is that moment when a Christ-follower or leader recognizes and moves to a new level of personal clarity. It's the moment when new insights change future realities. Breakthrough brings hope, and hope reacts in new courage.

Breakthrough in coaching is the by-product of a changing person, not just a changing situation. It is the result of new paradigms overcoming real world resistance and obstacles. The power of this kind of coaching is needed in the world today.

Why do so many illuminating experiences such as retreats, conferences, and powerful talks or sermons often dissolve with little life change? Usually it's because of the lack of alongside, relational support to help turn resistance and realities into ongoing, new behavior.

The IDEA Coaching Pathway was designed to better integrate the power and paradigms of leadership development into coaching. Each stepping stone in the path is sequenced into the coaching conversation to give coach and coachee the best opportunity possible to recognize God's purposes.

The coach's role in IDEA continues to be the one of facilitating and managing the discovery process. Most people who come to a coaching relationship are in need of answers. Their lives hover in the in-between, facing important decisions, knowing that there are crucial choices ahead. The answers are in the postures of asking vs. telling, listening vs. talking, and empowering vs. scripting found in good coaching. But these defining moments are about more than just career options. Instead, these moments are often about the individual's walk with God and their personal development as a follower of Christ.

There are four personal, leadership development moments that occur in the lives of all Christ-followers. Each of these defining moments will be reviewed showing how the IDEA path can bring greater breakthrough in your coaching.

TRANSITIONS

God often brings those in transition to the coaching relationship.

Transitions occur in the lives of marketplace leaders, vocational ministers, stay-at-home parents, students, the young and old, and the churched and non-churched. For Christ-followers, something more is occurring beyond just a change in career or the need for new scenery that often are the challenges of transitions.

God does some of his most important formation work during a time of transition. God sculpts clarity of life purpose, direction for the future, clarity of values, revealing of unique contribution, and so much more. The in-between times are important times.

Transitions are often characterized by confusion, indecision, isolation, a lack of motivation, lessening results, and struggles in knowing what's next. A Christ-follower knows that they cannot go back to where they were, but they are not sure which way forward is best. Transitions can last from three months to three years, and many Christ-followers get lost during a time of transition. Coaching is an incredible resource to help those in the midst of confusion and uncertainty process what is occurring and what God is at work doing.

The IDEA Coaching Pathway helps the coach to walk an individual through a time of transition.

- In **IDENTIFY**, the coach can normalize many of the emotions of a transition.

- In **DISCOVER**, the coachee has a safe place to unpack both the struggles and challenges of transition.

- In **EVALUATION**, the coach and coachee can look to what the Spirit is seeking to reveal and teach.

- In **ACT**, the coach can help the coachee make sure they are staying present and processing all that is occurring, as opposed to racing ahead.

It's important that a Christ-follower get all they can out of their transition.

Transitions do come to an end. Once they end most people typically move on to what's next. They take with them whatever they were able to process and gain.

Transitions are used by God to bring closure of one phase and greater alignment to God's continuing work. The stepping stones of the IDEA coaching pathway provide a helpful structure to process a time of transition.

Resource: Stuck! Navigating Life and Leadership Transitions *(Terry Walling). Includes coaching questions for those in transition.*

AWAKENING: CALLING

God uses coaching to help Christ-followers clarify their life calling.

Calling is about life direction. It occurs in each of our lives to summon us not to vocational ministry, but to a life of purpose and value much deeper than a job or title.

Each of us has been called (Ephesians 2:8-10, NIV). Life was never intended to be a mere day-to-day existence beginning somewhere in the 20s and extending to the end of the 60s. Instead, God moves in our lives and awakens our heart to God's greater purposes. God often uses what we call the Awakening Transition to get our attention.

Calling is about clarifying what's important (core values), what we desire from our relationship with God (being), and what God desires from our lives (doing).

IDEA Coaching Pathway provides a structured conversation that brings awareness to God's voice and work.

- In **IDENTIFY**, a coach helps surface the issues of day-to-day life, purpose and meaning.

- In **DISCOVER**, the coach can help a coachee uncover the work God has been doing in past development to point to issues of calling.

- In **EVALUATION**, the coach and coachee seek to discern God's desires and His imprint on the individual's influence.

- In **ACT**, the coachee can begin to chart next steps based upon the new clarity and set a new course direction.

Resource: Awakening: Awakening to God's Call *(Terry Walling, Kyle Walling, and Zack Curry). Includes coaching questions for those in the Awakening Transition.*

Focused Living Online Process: Clarifying Personal Calling: leaderbreakthru.com/focused-living

DECIDING: CONTRIBUTION

God uses coaching to help us decide when to say no in order to say yes.

The IDEA Coaching Pathway seeks to facilitate the alignment to God's purposes and plans for each of our lives. There will come a time when the good must give way to the best. Issues of calling give way to contribution. Decisions will need to be made. Coaching facilitates the defining moment called deciding.

You don't get to certainty without becoming convinced that God is at work leading your life. Contribution is about bringing clarity to God's shaping work by clarifying issues of role, core functions, and intentional choices that move us closer to the good works that God authored before time began (Ephesians 2:10). IDEA stepping stones help us discover and have the courage to follow God's lead.

> **"As the time approached for him to be taken up to heaven, Jesus resolutely set out for Jerusalem." – Luke 9:51 (NIV)**

Jesus made a series of choices en route to making the greatest contribution of all: his sacrifice on the cross and resurrection from the dead. Christ-followers need the safe place of a coaching relationship to say "no" to the good in order to say "yes" to the best.

The IDEA Coaching Pathway provides a structured conversation that brings awareness to God's forming work and our unique contributions.

- In **IDENTIFY**, a coach hears about the demands, the never-ending tasks, and the weight of responsibilities.

- In **DISCOVER**, the unfolding of the story reveals the deep longings for something more and the challenge of deciding what will not get done each day.

- In **EVALUATION**, the coach and coachee seek to determine God's best: of all the things that could be done, what does God want, and what should be done?

- In **ACT**, the coachee authors tangible steps that move beyond calling into unique contribution

Resources: Deciding: Clarifying Your Unique Contribution *(Terry Walling, Rick Williams, and Steve Hopkins). Includes coaching questions for those in the Deciding Transition.*

APEX Online Process: Clarifying Personal Contribution: leaderbreakthru.com/apex

FINISHING: CONVERGENCE

> *"I think it is right to refresh your memory as long as I live in the tent of this body, because I know that I will soon put it aside, as our Lord Jesus Christ has made clear to me. And I will make every effort to see that after my departure you will always be able to remember these things."* —2 Peter 1:13-15 (NIV)

Just like Peter, there comes a time when those who love Christ are called off the stage and into a time of stewardship. The focus shifts from continuing to produce the ministry to making every effort to see that others do it better.

> *"Few Leaders finish well. As few as one out of three." —Dr. J. Robert Clinton*

Leadership development language labels the end-game as the time for potential convergence. Convergence is when who you are intersects with what you do and you pass on the insights that God has entrusted to you to others. The focus for those at this stage of the journey is finding others who can take insights gained and do them better with greater Kingdom impact. It's letting those we see stand on our ceilings. Convergence is often ignited by the Finishing Transition.

The IDEA Coaching Pathway helps facilitate those discussions by providing the structure to the conversation that allows an individual to discover what has been entrusted and become intentional in one's action with regards to passing on the insights and skills.

- In **IDENTIFY**, a coach hears about the desires and struggles of knowing how to have influence without position.

- In **DISCOVER**, backstory lessons begin to emerge that point to insights and deposits that God has made into a life.

- In **EVALUATION**, the coach and coachee seek to determine what needs to be entrusted to others, as well as who and how the empowerment needs to occur.

- In **ACT** the coachee charts the steps, deciding to live intentionally for Christ to the end, and set in motion ways to outlive one's days.

Resources: Finishing: Making the Choices to Finish Well *(Terry Walling with Bob Grant). Includes coaching questions for those in the Finishing Transition.*

Resonance Online Process: Clarifying Personal Legacy: leaderbreakthru.com/resonance

CHAPTER 8
UTILIZING THE IDEA COACHING PATHWAY

The IDEA Coaching Pathway can be utilized in a variety of coaching situations. Depending on time limitations and the coaching expectations, IDEA can take from a few minutes up to an hour.

THREE APPLICATIONS

1. Coaching INTERACTIONS
IDEA can be used in periodic coaching encounters of 10-15 minute duration:
- Identify   2 min.
- Discover   7-8 min.
- Evaluate/Act   4-5 min.

2. Coaching CONVERSATIONS
IDEA can be used in situational coaching discussions of 20-30 minute duration:
- Identify   3–5 min.
- Discover   5-10 min.
- Evaluate   5-10 min.
- Act   3-5 min.

3. Coaching APPOINTMENTS
IDEA can be used in full coaching appointments of 45-60 minute duration:
- Identify   5–10 min.
- Discover   15-20 min.
- Evaluate   10-15 min.
- Act   10-15 min.

IDEA COACHING AND TRAINING

You can receive coaching from a certified Leader Breakthru coach who has been trained to utilize the IDEA Coaching Pathway. These coaches are passionate about coaching you and your development.

Find your coach at: leaderbreakthru.com/coaching

You can become a better coach by experiencing the **2-Day Coaching Skills Coach Training** utilizing the IDEA Coaching Pathway offered through Leader Breakthru. To locate the dates and location for a training event near you, contact Leader Breakthru: leaderbreakthru.com/coaching-skills

You can become a trainer-of-trainers and offer the 2-Day Coaching Skills to others by attending the **2+2 Coaching Skills and Certificate Training** from Leader Breakthru.

Leader Breakthru Certified coaches gain access to facilitate the training of coaches. You receive presenter resources that include notes, Power Point slides, and a special link for ordering the Coaching Skills workbook.

For more information: leaderbreakthru.com/coach-certificate

BUILDING A COACHING CULTURE

Developing a culture of coaching in your organization, mission agency, or local church takes time and commitment to not only train individuals to coach, but also to develop the mindset of coaching and resource and develop coaches that will help to sustain coaching for the long-haul.

Here is one leader's efforts to BUILD A COACHING CULTURE: *Bruce Pfadenhauer, Central Region Executive Director, Open Bible Churches*

After more than twenty-five years of leading local churches, I transitioned to overseeing pastors and churches. Leadership development is a vital part in both arenas and there are a number of strategies available. Coaching is our preferred method as it allows the leader to set the agenda, determine the outcome, and choose the action steps which raises the probability of the leader taking action.

We explored a number of coaching models and chose to partner with Leader Breakthru for the following reasons:

- *They provided capable leadership for our coaching development.*
- *They developed a workable coaching model.*
- *They created quality initial and ongoing training for our coaches.*
- *They designed excellent resources for our coaches.*

We began by sending a team of people to coaches' training which was fast-paced and thorough. It included adequate information, practical tools, and interactive participation. Our initial team was licensed and certified. Then we hosted Leader Breakthru for one of our conferences so that pastors and leaders could grasp the concept of coaching. We continued to host training events to add coaches.

Terry Walling coached and counseled our team as we began to shape our coaching system which included a website page to allow a leader to select his coach, complete a coaching agreement, and sign a confidentiality covenant. The webpage automatically linked the leader with their selected coach. Our coaches had access to Leader Breakthru's web resources as well as our own web resources. We budgeted funds for the continued training and resourcing of the coaches as well as paying coaches for their services.

We have recently added a layer of Lead Coaches whose primary role is to train, resource, and coach our coaches. A growing number of leaders are requesting coaching. The feedback has been positive in that leaders are being developed personally and professionally. As leaders advance in their development, the churches and organizations they lead will also rise. Leaders are called to be lifelong learners and coaching permits a leader to breakthrough, gain clarity, and grow as they serve in leading others.

Stepping Stones to building a coaching culture in your setting include could some key components and steps listed below.

Take the Coaching Approach

Training staff, board members, and key leaders in the power of "asking" vs. "telling" by asking questions. Offer a 2-hour workshop that introduces the IDEA Coaching Pathway plus practice in asking open questions.

Take a Coaching Posture

A next step beyond the *Coaching Approach* is to offer the 2-Day Coaching Skills to all staff and key ministry leaders. This can be accomplished by first attending the Leader Breakthru Coaching Skills training event, by taking your staff/ministry leaders to a 2-Day Coaching Skills Training near you. At this event you will receive tools, exercises and resources on how to introduce coaching and the IDEA Coaching Pathway to your leaders.

Building Your Own Coaching Culture

Very much like a system of small groups in a local church, your ability to sustain and multiply coaching in your ministry context is linked to the training, care, and development of your coaches.

In addition to building on the *Coaching Approach* and *Coaching Posture* (see above), this involves selecting a few coaches to become *Lead Coaches*.

Lead Coaches are those coaches who have been able to excel in the practice of coaching (behavior) and who recognize that coaching is one key expression of delivering who they are as a leader (passion). They are recognized by the coaching constituency as ones especially gifted as coaches, and who have gained the respect of their peers.

Developing Lead Coaches

Lead Coaches are a select group of coaches invited to move into the role of:

- Coaching the coaches
- Identifying, training, and developing future coaches
- Contributing insights into developing the future of the coaching system and the improvements needed to sustain a coaching culture

Lead Coaches should be postured within a system as those who are alongside coaches, helping to resource the quality of the coaching, as opposed to supervisors of the coaches.

The emerging coaching system does need a Director of Coaching who provides oversight and supervision to the system. *Lead Coaches* become his/her team as they system continues to grow and develop.

For more on developing a coaching culture in your setting, check out the "Organic Collective" at the Leader Breakthru website.

BOOKS WE RECOMMEND

Clinton, Robert J. (1988). *The Making of a Leader: Recognizing the Lessons and Stages of Leadership Development.* Colorado Springs: Nav Press.

Harkavay, Daniel: *Becoming a Coaching Leader* Grand Rapids: Baker Books.

Huckins, Jon and Yackley, Rob (2012). *Thin Places: Six Postures for Creating and Practicing Missional Community.* The House Studio

KImsey-House, Henry, Phil Sandahl, and Laura Whitworth. Co-Active Coaching: New Skills for Coaching people Toward Success in Work and Life. Palo Alto: Davies-Black Publishing

Ogne, Steve and Roehl, Tim (2008). *TransforMissional Coaching.* Nashville, TN. B&H Publishing.

Stoltzfus, Tony (2005). *Leadership Coaching: The Disciplines, Skills and Heart of a Christian Coach.* Virginia Beach, VA.

Walling, Terry. (2015 Edition). *Stuck! Navigating Life and Leadership Transitions*

Walling, Terry, Walling, Kyle, and Curry, Zack. (2015) *Awakening: Awakening to the Call of God.* Leader Breakthu/Create Space Independent Publishing

Webb, Keith. (2012)_*The COACH Model for Christian Leaders.* Active Results LLC.

Whitmore, Sir John (1992). *Coaching for Performance: GROWing Human Potential and Purpose (4th Edition) Nicholas Breely Publishing*

THE LEADERSHIP DEVELOPMENT SERIES

Leader Breakthru's Leadership Development Series consists of three books that take a closer look at the three significant transition moments that every Christ-follower will face. Each of these books can be used as a personal read, a small group resource or as a one-on-one coaching resource. For an introduction to the concept of transitions and an overview of these transitions, check out the book *Stuck! Navigating Life & Leadership Transitions*, by Terry Walling.

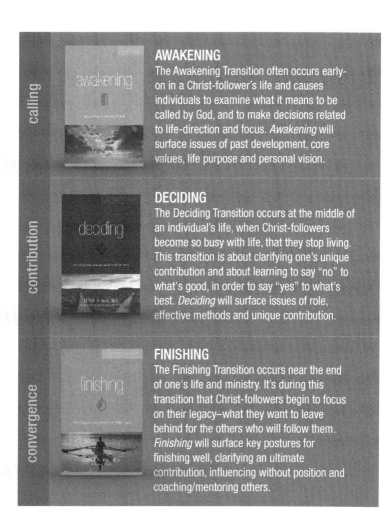

AWAKENING

The Awakening Transition often occurs early-on in a Christ-follower's life and causes individuals to examine what it means to be called by God, and to make decisions related to life-direction and focus. *Awakening* will surface issues of past development, core values, life purpose and personal vision.

DECIDING

The Deciding Transition occurs at the middle of an individual's life, when Christ-followers become so busy with life, that they stop living. This transition is about clarifying one's unique contribution and about learning to say "no" to what's good, in order to say "yes" to what's best. *Deciding* will surface issues of role, effective methods and unique contribution.

FINISHING

The Finishing Transition occurs near the end of one's life and ministry. It's during this transition that Christ-followers begin to focus on their legacy—what they want to leave behind for the others who will follow them. *Finishing* will surface key postures for finishing well, clarifying an ultimate contribution, influencing without position and coaching/mentoring others.

3 Core Processes™

Leader Breakthru offers three core, personal development processes that are designed to guide the on-going development of a Christ-follower. Together they comprise a leadership development system for churches, missions, ministries and organizations.

If you'd like more information about these processes, would like to go through one of the processes online, or would like to gain a license to facilitate one of the processes in your context, please visit: leaderbreakthru.com

FOCUSED LIVING

The Focused Living Process consists of six-sessions related to clarifying life direction and personal calling. This process helps leaders and all Christ-followers gain perspective through the development of core values, a statement of being (life purpose) and a statement of doing (personal vision).

APEX

The APEX Process consists of eight-sessions that bring greater clarity to a Christ-follower's unique, personal contribution. This process will help individuals discover issues related to their major role and effective methods, and will provide a decision-making grid called a "Personal Life Mandate" that will help to guide any choices that lay ahead.

RESONANCE

The Resonance Process is a series of three preparatory meetings and three strategic discussions by those who love Christ and desire to finish well. This process helps Christ-followers to clarify how to have influence without position, empower others and leave behind a godly legacy.

calling

contribution

convergence

ABOUT THE AUTHOR

Terry Walling brings over 30 years of coaching and training experience and 14 years of pastoral staff experience to the creation of this resource.

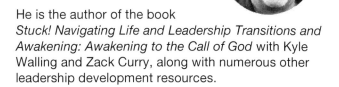

He is the author of the book *Stuck! Navigating Life and Leadership Transitions and Awakening: Awakening to the Call of God* with Kyle Walling and Zack Curry, along with numerous other leadership development resources.

Terry's passion, and that of Leader Breakthru, is to resource and coach breakthrough in the lives leaders and their development, empowering them toward a greater Kingdom contribution for Christ's Kingdom.

Terry is founder and President of Leader Breakthru. He is a speaker, trainer, and lead facilitator of the Leader Breakthru Coaching Skills and Certificate training program. Terry also teaches in the Doctor of Ministry program at Fuller Theological Seminary and is Director of Fuller's DMin. Mentoring Program.

For more information regarding Terry Walling and the ministry of Leader Breakthru, visit: leaderbreakthru.com

53579675R00050

Made in the USA
San Bernardino, CA
21 September 2017